100 Calorie Snacks

Recipes and References for Everyday Snack Attacks

Printed in the United States of America
by G&R Publishing Co.

Published By:

507 Industrial Street
Waverly, IA 50677

ISBN-13: 978-1-56383-296-3
ISBN-10: 1-56383-296-8
Item #7103

TABLE OF CONTENTS

THE SKINNY ON SNACKS

Having a snack attack?

It's hard to make it through the day without nibbling on snacks between meals. Let's face it: sometimes that nibbling is what gets us through the day. And sometimes, it's what gets us in trouble.

Eating healthy snacks is almost as important as eating three healthy meals a day. Making sure you eat healthy, well-rounded snacks helps avoid the intake of unwanted calories, and also gives a much-needed burst of mid-day energy.

This book is packed with recipes for healthy, well-balanced snacks that are 100 calories or less. Since food portions, brands and packaging can vary, calories and fat content listed are an estimate. But rest assured: all these snacks are as close to 100 calories or less as you can get.

Now you can treat yourself with guilt-free snacks that satisfy even the sweetest and saltiest of cravings.

What are calories?

A calorie is a unit of measurement, but it doesn't measure length or weight. A calorie is actually a unit of energy. For example, when you read a portion of food contains 100 calories, the measurement is describing how much energy you get from eating that particular portion of food.

Calories are very important – your body needs them for energy, but eating too many calories can lead to weight gain. This is why it's important to count calories when you are trying to lose or maintain your weight. If you take in more calories than you burn, you will gain weight. If you take in fewer calories than you burn, you will lose weight. If you balance the two, you will maintain your weight.

Calories should not be cut back so much that your energy needs are not met. The number of calories you need depends primarily on your age, gender and activity level. Consult a doctor or nutritionist to determine what your calorie intake should be.

The combination of counting calories and eating foods rich in nutrients is the best way to maintain your weight and live a healthy lifestyle.

Eat healthy. Live healthy. Be healthy.

Choosing foods and portions sensibly is critical to controlling your calorie intake and your weight.

THE SKINNY ON SNACKS

According to the United States Department of Agriculture (USDA), many Americans are becoming overweight or obese. These conditions can lead to chronic diseases, such as high blood pressure, diabetes, stroke, cancer and diseases of the gallbladder, heart and lungs. Such diseases can reduce the quality of life and sometimes lead to premature death.

Determining a healthy weight for you will help establish your eating plan. According to the National Institutes of Health (NIH), for adults, a healthy weight is defined as the appropriate weight in relation to height. Body Mass Index (BMI) is commonly used to classify weight as "healthy" or "unhealthy". BMI is the ratio of a person's weight to height. Similar to the information above, the USDA states the link between BMI and health shows that overweight or obese people are more likely than those at healthy weights to have medical problems.

Use the NIH table below to determine your BMI and find out if your current weight is healthy.*

NATIONAL INSTITUTES OF HEALTH BMI TABLE

	Healthy Weight						Overweight					Obese					
BMI	19	20	21	22	23	24	25	26	27	28	29	30	31	32	33	34	35
Height								*Body Weight (pounds)*									
4' 10"	91	96	100	105	110	115	119	124	129	134	138	143	148	153	158	162	167
4' 11"	94	99	104	109	114	119	124	128	133	138	143	148	153	158	163	168	173
5' 0"	97	102	107	112	118	123	128	133	138	143	148	153	158	163	168	174	179
5' 1"	100	106	111	116	122	127	132	137	143	148	153	158	164	169	174	180	185
5' 2"	104	109	115	120	126	131	136	142	147	153	158	164	169	175	180	186	191
5' 3"	107	113	118	124	130	135	141	146	152	158	163	169	175	180	186	191	197
5' 4"	110	116	122	128	134	140	145	151	157	163	169	174	180	186	192	197	204
5' 5"	114	120	126	132	138	144	150	156	162	168	174	180	186	192	198	204	210
5' 6"	118	124	130	136	142	148	155	161	167	173	179	186	192	198	204	210	216
5' 7"	121	127	134	140	146	153	159	166	172	178	185	191	198	204	211	217	223
5' 8"	125	131	138	144	151	158	164	171	177	184	190	197	203	210	216	223	230
5' 9"	128	135	142	149	155	162	169	176	182	189	196	203	209	216	223	230	236
5' 10"	132	139	146	153	160	167	174	181	188	195	202	209	216	222	229	236	243
5' 11"	136	143	150	157	165	172	179	186	193	200	208	215	222	229	236	243	250
6' 0"	140	147	154	162	169	177	184	191	199	206	213	221	228	235	242	250	258
6' 1"	144	151	159	166	174	182	189	197	204	212	219	227	235	242	250	257	265
6' 2"	148	155	163	171	179	186	194	202	210	218	225	233	241	249	256	264	272
6' 3"	152	160	168	176	184	192	200	208	216	224	232	240	248	256	264	272	279
6' 4"	156	164	172	180	189	197	205	213	221	230	238	246	254	263	271	279	287

*Please note that although BMI provides a good measure of obesity, it does not take into account features that make up a person's total body weight, such as proportions of bone, muscle and fat. For example, BMI should not be used to determine the obesity of athletes with well-developed muscles and dense bones, or persons with a large body frame that might have little fat. BMI is not a good indication in growing children and pregnant women either.

If you are unsure about your weight category according to your BMI, it is best to discuss your weight and corresponding eating plan with a doctor or nutritionist.

Once you've determined your lifestyle goals and plan for maintaining a healthy weight, you can start choosing foods that fit your needs.

A little exercise always helps!

According to the USDA, physical activity and nutrition work together for improved health. Activity increases the amount of calories you use, and in turn, helps you reach and/or maintain a healthy weight.

There are two types of physical activity that promote a healthy lifestyle: aerobic activity and activities for strength and flexibility. Aerobic activity increases your heart rate, speeds up your breathing and assists in cardiovascular fitness. Strength and flexibility activities help build and maintain bones and joints.

Adults should practice some sort of physical activity for 30 minutes a day for most days, if not every day of the week.

Physical activities you can make part of your daily routine:

- Take the stairs instead of the elevator
- Mow the lawn with a push mower instead of a riding mower
- Push a stroller
- Rake the leaves
- Clean the house
- Ride a bike or walk to work

THE SKINNY ON SNACKS

Other fun activities to try:

- Swimming or water aerobics
- Canoeing
- Cross-country skiing
- Ballroom dancing
- Golf
- Yoga

You should find a good balance between physical activity and the food you eat. You need to eat enough calories to meet your energy needs. The body needs some calories just to operate – to keep the lungs working and heart beating. If you cut back on calories too much, your system will slow down and could even shut down. In other words, don't starve yourself in order to lose weight and don't overexert yourself when you haven't had very much to eat.

Pack and Go Snacks

Throughout *100 Calorie Snacks* you will find several recipes with the Pack and Go Snack icon. These tasty treats are great for taking to work, tossing in your purse, backpack or briefcase, or packing in your lunch, cooler or thermos. Taking along some snacks for your busy day makes it easier to avoid the lure of vending machines, drive-thrus and snack bars.

100 Calorie Quick Lists

BEVERAGES

Beverages	Size	Calories
Tomato Juice (average of all brands)	1 cup	50
Michelob ULTRA Beer	12 oz. can	95
Miller Lite Beer	12 oz. can	96
Olympia Gold Light Beer	12 oz. can	70
Minute Maid Pulp Free Orange Juice	¾ cup	83
Tropicana No Pulp Orange Juice	¾ cup	83
Fat-free Skim Milk	1 cup	90

PROTEIN & NUTS

Protein & Nuts	Size	Calories
Sunflower Seeds, dry roasted & shelled	2 T.	90
Hard-boiled Egg	1 egg	78
Peanut Butter	1 T.	95
Almonds, whole	12 nuts	84
Pine Nuts	84 nuts	96
Pecan Halves	10 nuts	100
Pistachio Nuts	20 nuts	80
Soy Nuts	2 T.	97
Cashew Pieces	2 T.	98
Walnut Halves	6 nuts	80

DAIRY

Dairy	Size	Calories
Yoplait Light Yogurt, Fruit Flavors	6 oz.	90 to 100
Dannon Light 'n Fit Creamy 0% Fat Yogurt, Fruit Flavors	6 oz.	60 to 90
Cottage Cheese, 1% Fat	½ cup	82
Mozzarella String Cheese	1 oz.	80
Mozzarella String Cheese, 2% Milk	1 oz.	70
Kraft American Cheese Singles	1 slice	70
Kraft Cheese Cubes, Colby & Monterey Jack	6 cubes	90

SWEETS

Sweets	Size	Calories
Hunt's Fat Free and No Sugar Added Pudding Snack Packs, all flavors	1 pkg.	90 or less
Jello Sugar Free Gelatin Cups, all flavors	1 pkg.	10
Twix Fun Size	1 pkg.	80
M&M's Fun Size	1 pkg.	100
Almond Joy Snack Size	1 pkg.	91
Baby Ruth Fun Size	1 pkg.	85
Butterfinger Fun Size	1 pkg.	100
Hershey's Milk Chocolate Bar Snack Size	1 pkg.	90
Junior Mints	8 candies	85
Kit Kat Snack Size	1 pkg.	80
Milky Way Fun Size	1 pkg.	75
Kellogg's Rice Krispies Treats Original Bar	1 pkg.	90
Snickers Fun Size	1 pkg.	80
Starbursts Fruit Chews	5 pieces	100
Twizzlers Cherry Bites	12 pieces	94
Jelly Belly Jelly Beans, any flavor	25 pieces	100
Tootsie Pop	1 sucker	60
Tootsie Miniature Pop	1 sucker	17
Blow Pop	1 sucker	60
Dum Dum Pop	1 sucker	26
Werther's Original Butter Candies	3 pieces	60
Werther's Original Butter Candies Sugar-Free	5 pieces	40
Brach's Butterscotch Disks	3 candies	70
Breyers Fat-Free French Chocolate Ice Cream	½ cup	90
Breyers Fat-Free Creamy Vanilla Ice Cream	½ cup	90
Breyers No Sugar Added Chocolate Fudge Brownie Ice Cream	½ cup	90
Breyers No Sugar Added Vanilla Ice Cream	½ cup	80
Edy's Slow Churned No Sugar Added Vanilla Ice Cream	½ cup	90
Edy's/Dreyer's Slow Churned No Sugar Added French Vanilla Ice Cream	½ cup	100

Sweets	Size	Calories
Edy's/Dreyer's Slow Churned No Sugar Added Vanilla Chocolate Swirl Ice Cream	½ cup	100
Edy's/Dreyer's Slow Churned No Sugar Added Neapolitan Ice Cream	½ cup	90
Edy's/Dreyer's Slow Churned No Sugar Added Chocolate Ice Cream	½ cup	95
Edy's/Dreyer's Slow Churned No Sugar Added Coffee Ice Cream	½ cup	90
Archway Fat-Free Sugar Cookies	1 cookie	71
Archway Ginger Snaps	3 cookies	90
Nabisco Nilla Wafers	5 cookies	88
Nabisco Nilla Wafers Reduced-Fat	7 cookies	97
Fat-Free Fig Newtons	2 bars	90
Teddy Grahams, all varieties	18 pieces	98
Dairy Queen Fudge Bar	1 bar	50
Dairy Queen Vanilla Orange Bar	1 bar	50
Dairy Queen Starkiss Bar	1 bar	80
Baskin-Robbins Cafe Mocha Nonfat Soft Serve Yogurt	½ cup	90
Baskin-Robbins Chocolate No Sugar Added Nonfat Soft Serve Yogurt	½ cup	80
Baskin-Robbins Vanilla No Sugar Added Nonfat Soft Serve Yogurt	½ cup	90

For a yummy sorbet, simply freeze these juices until slushy!

Sweets	Size	Calories
Minute Maid Pulp Free Orange Juice	¾ cup	83
Minute Maid Lemonade	¾ cup	83
Minute Maid Raspberry Lemonade	¾ cup	83
Minute Maid Cherry Lemonade	¾ cup	90

GRAINS

Grains	Size	Calories
Corn Chex Creal	½ cup	60
Rice Chex Cereal	½ cup	50
Corn Pops Cereal	½ cup	60
Cheerios Cereal	½ cup	100
Apple Cinnamon Cheerios Cereal	½ cup	60
Honey Nut Cheerios Cereal	½ cup	74
Multigrain Cheerios Cereal	½ cup	60
Cinnamon Toast Crunch Cereal	½ cup	87
Golden Grahams Cereal	½ cup	80
Kix Cereal	¾ cup	66
Life Cereal	½ cup	80
Rice Cakes	1 cake	35
Keebler Club Crackers	5 crackers	88
Town House Original Crackers	6 crackers	96
Ritz Crackers	6 crackers	96
Toasted Buttercrisp, Onion or Sesame Crackers	6 crackers	96
Nabisco Cheese Nips	19 crackers	99
Nabisco Reduced-Fat Cheese Nips	20 crackers	84
Cheez-It Crisps	20 crackers	84
Cheese-It Reduced-Fat Crackers	20 crackers	90
Honey Maid Grahams Cinnamon Sticks	10 sticks	93
Nabisco or Zesta Saltines	8 crackers	96
Wheat Thins Originals	10 crackers	88
Goldfish Crackers	35 pieces	89
Light Microwave Popcorn (average of all brands)	2 cups	40 to 60
Baked Original Ruffles	8 chips	96
Wheatables Original, Honey Wheat or Seven Grain	12 crackers	99
Quaker Oats Quakes (all varieties)	11 to 13 pieces	91 to 98
Special K Cereal Bar (all varieties)	1 bar	90
Quaker Oats Regular Oatmeal Microwave Packet (made with water)	1 packet	100

Grains	Size	Calories
Baked Lays Original Potato Chips	10 chips	100
Baked Lays Sour Cream & Onion Potato Chips	10 chips	100
Sun Chips (all varieties)	10 chips	86 to 94
Tostitos Baked Scoops	12 chips	96
Bugles Original Flavor	⅔ cup	80

VEGGIES

Veggies	Size	Calories
Tomato	1 medium	25
Cherry Tomatoes	1 cup	27
Bell Peppers	½ cup	20
Celery	1 stalk	10
Cucumber	½ cup	10
Broccoli	1 cup	31
Baby Carrots	15 medium	60
Cauliflower	1 cup	25
Radishes	10 pieces	10
Edamame, steamed	½ cup	95
Artichoke	1 medium	25
Sugar Snap Peas	1 cup	26
Vlasic or Claussen Dill Pickle Spears	5 spears	25
Vlasic Baby Dill Pickles	10 baby pickles	50
Vlasic Sweet Gherkins Pickles	3 pickles	40

FRUITS

Fresh Fruits	Size	Calories
Apple	1 medium (⅓ lb.)	75
Apricot	1 medium (2 oz.)	25
Banana	1 small (¼ lb.)	90
Blackberries	1 cup	70
Blueberries	1 cup	80
Canned Mandarin Oranges	1 cup	92
Cantaloupe	1 cup	55
Clementine	2 medium (2.5 oz.)	70
Pineapple	1 cup	76
Grapes	1 cup	62
Honeydew	1 cup	60
Kiwifruit	1 medium	45
Large Black Olives	10	60
Large Stuffed Green Olives	10	60
Mandarin Orange	1 medium (¼ lb.)	50
Nectarine	1 medium (¼ lb.)	65
Orange	1 medium	80
Papaya	1 cup	60
Peach	1 medium (¼ lb.)	45
Pear	1 medium (6 oz.)	95
Plum	1 medium	45
Raspberries	1 cup	60
Strawberries	1 cup	43
Tangerine	1 medium	50
Watermelon	1 cup	45

Dried Fruits	Size	Calories
Dried Apricots	¼ cup	73
Prunes	5 medium	100
Dried Apples	6 rings	90
Sweetened Dried Cranberries	¼ cup	98
Raisins	3 T.	98

Canned Fruits	Size	Calories
Apricots in Light Syrup	½ cup	60
Peaches in Juice	½ cup	60
Pears in Juice	½ cup	60
Pineapple Tidbits in Juice	½ cup	70

Snack Cups	Size	Calories
Del Monte Diced Pears	1-4 oz. snack cup	80
Dole Diced Pears	1-4 oz. snack cup	70
Del Monte Tropical Fruit	1-4 oz. snack cup	70
Dole Tropical Fruit	1-4 oz. snack cup	80
Del Monte Mixed Fruit	1-4 oz. snack cup	70
Dole Mixed Fruit	1-4 oz. snack cup	80
Mandarin Oranges	1-4 oz. snack cup	70
Diced Peaches	1-4 oz. snack cup	70
Del Monte Pineapple Tidbits	1-4 oz. snack cup	70
Dole Pineapple Tidbits	1-4 oz. snack cup	60
Del Monte Cherry Mixed Fruit	1-4 oz. snack cup	70
Fruit in Gel	1-4.3 to 4.5 oz. snack cup	60 to 90
Applesauce	1-4 oz. snack cup	80 to 100
Chunky Applesauce	1-4 oz. snack cup	100
Cinnamon Applesauce	1-4 oz. snack cup	80 to 100
Lite Applesauce	1-4 oz. snack cup	50
Natural Applesauce	1-4 oz. snack cup	50
Strawberry Applesauce	1-4 oz. snack cup	90

QUICK GUIDE TO ARTIFICIAL SWEETENERS

Equal Spoonful

Equal Spoonful contains zero calories and works well with food and drink recipes. However, it cannot be used in baked recipes. It comes in a 2- or 4-ounce container and can be measured by the spoonful like sugar.

SPLENDA No Calorie Sweetener, Granular

Splenda Granular contains zero calories. It measures and pours just like sugar and can be used almost anywhere sugar is used, including cooking and baking. It's available in packages containing the sweetness equivalent of one- and two-pound boxes of sugar and a baker's bag containing the sweetness equivalent to five pounds of sugar.

NutraSweet Spoonful

Similar to Equal Granular, NutraSweet Spoonful can be measured spoon-for-spoon like real sugar, but NutraSweet Spoonful, at two calories per teaspoon, has only ⅛ the calories of sugar. Like Equal Spoonful, NutraSweet Spoonful cannot be used in traditional baked recipes.

Equal Sugar Lite

Equal Sugar Lite has 8 calories per teaspoon and 0 grams of fat. It is a blend of real sugar and no-calorie sweeteners that provide half the calories and carbohydrates of regular sugar while measuring and baking like traditional sugar.

Crunchy
Munchies

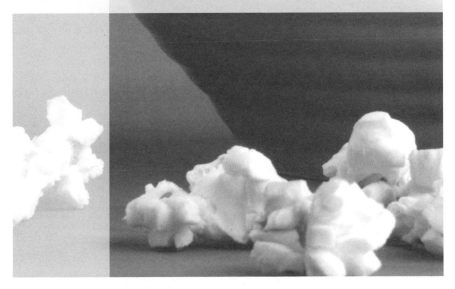

Honey Peanut Butter Popcorn Balls

Makes 9 popcorn balls

5 C. popped popcorn
¼ C. honey
¼ C. creamy peanut butter

Place popped popcorn in a large pan and warm in the oven at a temperature of 250°. In a small saucepan over medium heat, boil honey for 1 to 2 minutes. Reduce heat and add peanut butter immediately; stir until well combined. Drizzle honey mixture over popcorn and stir to coat well. Tear off nine 10″ square sheets of waxed paper. Place slightly more than ½ cup of popcorn on the center of each square. Fold corners around the popcorn and twist at the top; shape popcorn into a ball. Repeat with remaining popcorn and paper to make eight more balls. Store popcorn balls in an airtight container. Peel waxed paper from popcorn balls to serve.

Serving size: *1 popcorn ball*
Calories: *98*
Fat: *4 g*

Italian Seasoned Munchy Mix

Makes 9 cups

¼ C. unpopped popcorn
2 C. toasted oat cereal
2 C. bite-sized shredded wheat squares
2 T. margarine, melted
¼ C. grated Parmesan cheese
1 T. dry Italian salad dressing mix

Preheat oven to 300°. In a heavy skillet or saucepan over medium-low heat, pop popcorn using little oil. Or, pop popcorn in a hot-air popper. Cover skillet or saucepan and shake until completely popped. In a 9 x 13″ baking pan, combine popcorn, oat cereal and wheat squares. Bake in the oven for 5 minutes. Remove from oven and drizzle with melted margarine. In a small bowl, combine Parmesan cheese and Italian salad dressing mix. Sprinkle the cheese mixture over the popcorn and stir until snack mix is well coated. Serve munchy mix warm.

Serving size: *½ cup*
Calories: *60*
Fat: *2 g*

Sweet Caramel
Popcorn

Makes 6 cups

6 C. popped popcorn
2 T. margarine
2 T. honey

Preheat oven to 325°. Spread popcorn evenly over a large shallow baking pan. In a small saucepan, melt margarine with honey. Pour mixture over popcorn; stir to coat well. Bake in the oven for 8 to 10 minutes; stir often. Let cool slightly before serving. Store popcorn in an airtight container.

Serving size: ¾ cup
Calories: 81
Fat: 3 g

Feel the Burn!

Go ahead and take the escalator, but climb the stairs while you ride. You'll get to the top sooner and just 5 minutes of stair climbing burns 144 calories.

Chocolate Lovers' Popcorn

Makes 6 cups

6 C. popped popcorn
1 T. margarine
2 T. light corn syrup
1 T. unsweetened cocoa powder
1½ T. skim milk
⅛ tsp. salt

Place popped popcorn in a shallow baking pan and warm in oven at a temperature of 250° while making chocolate sauce. In a small saucepan over low heat, melt margarine. Add corn syrup, cocoa powder, milk and salt; stir until well blended and mixture is hot. Pour chocolate mixture over popcorn. Stir well to coat all pieces before serving.

Serving size: *1 cup*
Calories: *94*
Fat: *2 g*

Parmesan Pizza Popcorn

Makes 2 cups

⅓ C. unpopped popcorn
⅓ C. butter, melted
1 T. pizza seasoning
½ C. grated Parmesan cheese

In a heavy skillet or saucepan over medium high heat, pop popcorn in butter. Cover skillet or saucepan and shake until completely popped. Sprinkle pizza seasoning and Parmesan cheese over popcorn; stir to coat well. Serve popcorn warm.

Serving size: *½ cup*
Calories: *58*
Fat: *4 g*

Black Bean
Tortilla Cups

Makes 16 tortilla cups

4 (8″) fat-free tortillas, cut into quarters
1 medium onion, grated
1 (16 oz.) can black beans, rinsed and drained
1 (8 oz.) jar chunky salsa
Fat-free sour cream, optional
Chopped fresh cilantro, optional

Preheat oven to 350°. Spray 16 muffin cups with nonstick cooking spray. Place one tortilla quarter into the bottom of each muffin cup. Layer some of the onion, black beans and salsa into each prepared muffin cup. Bake in the oven for 8 to 10 minutes or until heated through. To serve, garnish with sour cream and cilantro if desired.

Serving size: *1 tortilla cup*
Calories: 56
Fat: *1 g*

PB & J Popcorn

6 C. popped popcorn
1½ T. margarine
1 T. peanut butter
2 tsp. low-sugar fruit spread

Place popped popcorn in a shallow baking pan and warm in oven at a temperature of 250° while making peanut butter and jelly topping. In a small saucepan over low heat, melt margarine. Stir in peanut butter and fruit spread. Pour mixture over warm popcorn and stir to coat well. Serve popcorn immediately.

Serving size: 1 cup
Calories: 100
Fat: 4 g

Chili Cheese Popcorn

Makes 8 cups

3 T. margarine
½ tsp. chili powder
½ tsp. garlic salt
¼ tsp. onion powder
8 C. popped popcorn
½ C. grated Parmesan cheese

In a small saucepan over low heat, melt margarine. Add chili powder, garlic salt and onion powder; stir well. Pour margarine mixture over popped popcorn. Sprinkle with Parmesan cheese and toss to coat well before serving.

Serving size: *1 cup*
Calories: *90*
Fat: *6.5 g*

Toasted Oat Trail Mix

Makes 3 cups

2 C. round whole-grain toasted oat cereal
¼ C. dried cranberries
¼ C. golden raisins
¼ C. crumbled banana chips
1 T. peanuts

In a medium bowl, combine toasted oat cereal, cranberries, raisins, banana chips and peanuts. Stir well to combine. Serve immediately or store in a resealable plastic bag.

Serving size: *½ cup*
Calories: *94*
Fat: *2.7 g*

Feel the Burn!

Boogie down and kick up your heels. About 20 minutes of dancing at a moderate pace will burn 100 calories.

Strawberry
Swirl Popcorn

Makes 6 cups

6 C. popped popcorn
2½ T. margarine
1 tsp. sugar-free strawberry flavored gelatin

Place popped popcorn in a shallow baking pan and warm in oven at a temperature of 250°. In a small saucepan over low heat, melt margarine. Let cool slightly. Stir in strawberry gelatin. Quickly pour mixture over popcorn and toss well to coat before serving.

Serving size: *½ cup*
Calories: *56*
Fat: *3 g*

Spicy Microwave Popcorn

Makes 6 to 8 cups

1 (3.5 oz.) bag microwave popcorn
2 T. butter or margarine
2 T. spicy brown mustard
2 tsp. chili powder
2 tsp. hot pepper sauce

Preheat oven to 375°. Pop microwave popcorn as directed on package. In a large microwave-safe bowl, combine butter or margarine, mustard, chili powder and hot pepper sauce. Cook, uncovered, in the microwave on high power for 45 seconds or until butter or margarine is melted; stir once. Add popcorn to butter mixture and stir until well coated. Spread coated popcorn onto a shallow baking pan. Bake in the oven for 8 to 10 minutes or until popcorn coating slightly browns. Remove from oven and let cool completely before serving. Store in a large resealable plastic bag for up to three days.

Serving size: *½ cup*
Calories: *74*
Fat: *5 g*

Romano Phyllo Mini Sticks

Makes 48 cups

1 C. grated Romano cheese
1 T. pepper
12 (12 x 16″) sheets fresh or frozen phyllo, thawed
5 T. butter or margarine, melted

Preheat oven to 450°. In a small bowl, combine Romano cheese and pepper. Place one phyllo sheet on waxed paper and lightly brush with some of the melted butter or margarine. Cover remaining sheets with plastic wrap to prevent drying out until ready to be used. Sprinkle 1 rounded tablespoon of cheese mixture over phyllo sheet. Fold sheet in half crosswise. Starting from open side, roll phyllo up tightly, similar to a jelly roll, toward the folded side. Cut crosswise into four 3″ sticks. Place sticks 1″ apart, seam side down, on a large baking sheet. Brush with some more of the melted butter or margarine. Repeat process with remaining phyllo sheets and cheese. Bake in the oven for 5 to 7 minutes or until golden brown. Serve sticks warm or at room temperature.

Serving size: *2 sticks*
Calories: *70*
Fat: *4 g*

Tasty Tip

Romano Phyllo Mini Sticks taste great as a dipper with any low-calorie sauce or dip.

Lemon-Pepper Cracker Crisps

Makes 36 crisps

2¼ C. flour
2¼ tsp. kosher salt, divided
1½ tsp. baking powder
¼ tsp. pepper
1 C. chopped fresh parsley
1 T. fresh grated lemon peel
¾ C. water
2 T. olive oil, divided

In a medium bowl, combine flour, 2 teaspoons kosher salt, baking powder and pepper. Add parsley and lemon peel; mix until well combined. Add water and, using a wooden spoon, stir until dough forms a ball. Knead dough by hand for 2 minutes or until smooth. Divide dough in half and cover each portion with plastic wrap; let set for 10 minutes. Preheat oven to 350°. Using a floured rolling pin, on a lightly floured surface roll one dough half into a thin rectangle about 12 x 18˝. Cut dough in half lengthwise to form two rectangles. Cut each rectangle crosswise into 2˝ wide strips. Place strips 1˝ apart on two ungreased baking sheets and let set for 10 minutes. Lightly brush strips with 1 tablespoon olive oil and sprinkle with some of the remaining salt. Bake in the oven for 15 to 18 minutes or until lightly browned. Rotate baking sheets halfway through cooking time. Remove from oven and transfer to wire racks to cool. Repeat process with remaining dough half. Store cracker crisps in an airtight container for up to two weeks.

Serving size: *2 cracker crisps*
Calories: *70*
Fat: *2 g*

Classic Party Mix

Makes 25 cups

¼ C. Worcestershire sauce
¼ C. butter or margarine
2 T. brown sugar
1½ tsp. salt
½ to 1 tsp. cayenne pepper
12 C. popped popcorn
1 (12 oz.) pkg. toasted corn cereal squares
1 (8 to 10 oz.) pkg. thin pretzel sticks

Preheat oven to 300°. In a 1-quart saucepan over low heat, combine Worcestershire sauce, butter, brown sugar, salt and cayenne pepper; stir often until butter has melted. Place half the popped popcorn, half the cereal and half the pretzels in a large roasting pan; toss with half the Worcestershire sauce mixture. Bake in the oven for 30 minutes; stir once halfway through. Remove from oven and transfer to a large bowl to cool. Repeat baking procedure with remaining popcorn, cereal, pretzels and Worcestershire sauce mixture.

Serving size: *½ cup*
Calories: *65*
Fat: *1 g*

Seeded Phyllo Sticks

Makes 48 sticks

⅓ C. sesame seeds
⅓ C. poppy seeds
½ tsp. salt
12 (12 x 16″) sheets fresh or frozen phyllo, thawed
5 T. butter or margarine, melted

In a large cup, combine sesame seeds, poppy seeds and salt. Place one phyllo sheet on waxed paper and lightly brush with some of the melted butter or margarine. Cover remaining sheets with plastic wrap to prevent drying out until ready to be used. Sprinkle 1 rounded tablespoon of seed mixture over phyllo sheet. Fold sheet in half crosswise. Starting from the longer open side, roll phyllo up tightly, similar to a jelly roll, toward the folded side. Cut crosswise into four 3″ sticks. Place sticks 1″ apart, seam side down, on a large baking sheet. Brush with some more of the melted butter or margarine. Repeat process with remaining phyllo sheets and seed mixture. Bake in the oven for 5 to 7 minutes or until golden brown. Serve sticks warm or at room temperature.

Serving size: *2 sticks*
Calories: *70*
Fat: *4 g*

Tasty Tip

Seeded Phyllo Sticks taste great as a dipper with any low-calorie sauce or dip.

Dips & Dippers

Please note each recipe in this section is 100 calories or less. Serving suggestions have been provided, however when pairing these recipes with one of the recommended dips or dippers, the complete snack may exceed 100 calories.

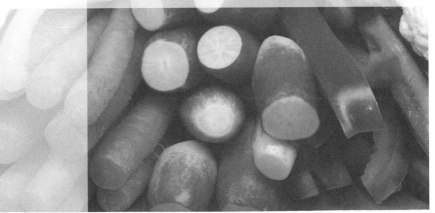

Corny Black Bean Dip

Makes 3 cups

1 (15 oz.) can black beans, rinsed and drained
2 C. cooked fresh, frozen or canned corn
2 green onions, sliced
½ C. plain nonfat yogurt
½ tsp. thyme
½ tsp. chili powder
Pepper to taste

Place beans, corn, green onions, yogurt, thyme, chili powder and pepper in a blender. Blend for 20 seconds or until mixture is smooth. Transfer to a serving bowl and serve with homemade baked tortilla chips. See page 31 for tortilla chip recipe.

Serving size: *¼ cup*
Calories: *68*
Fat: *0 g*

Baked Tortilla Chips

Makes 48 chips

6 corn tortillas
1 C. water
Chili powder to taste

Preheat oven to 450°. Quickly dip each tortilla in water to help chips crisp during baking. Cut each tortilla into eight wedges. Place the wedges on an ungreased baking sheet and spread them out. Sprinkle with chili powder; bake in the oven for 5 to 8 minutes or until chips are crisp. Remove from oven and spread baked chips over wire racks to cool before serving.

Serving size: *13 tortilla chips*
Calories: *91*
Fat: *1.6 g*

Feel the Burn!

Have some dirty laundry? About 25 minutes of ironing will burn more than 100 calories.

Broccoli Mushroom Dip

Makes 3 cups

2 C. chopped broccoli
1 garlic clove, minced
1 small onion, chopped
¼ lb. chopped mushrooms
2 tsp. canola or corn oil
1 C. low-fat cottage cheese
Pinch of pepper

Cook broccoli until tender-crisp. Drain water from broccoli and set aside. In a small skillet over medium-high heat, cook garlic, onion and mushrooms in canola or corn oil. Cook for 5 minutes or until onion is tender. Using a food processor or blender, process cottage cheese until smooth. Add broccoli, garlic, onion, mushrooms and pepper; process until well combined. Serve with various vegetables or as a topping for baked potatoes. To store, cover and refrigerate.

Serving size: *¼ cup*
Calories: *29*
Fat: *1 g*

Low Calorie Ranch Dressing-Dip

1 C. light or fat-free mayonnaise

2 T. lemon juice

2 T. chopped fresh parsley

2 T. chopped green onion

3 packets Equal sweetener

1 T. Dijon mustard

1½ tsp. minced fresh garlic

¼ tsp. salt

¾ C. buttermilk

In a medium bowl, combine mayonnaise, lemon juice, parsley, green onion, Equal sweetener, Dijon mustard, garlic and salt; stir with a wire whisk until well blended. Whisk in buttermilk. Cover and refrigerate for 1 to 2 hours. Serve with fresh vegetables or as dressing for a salad.

Serving size: *3 tablespoons*
Calories: *85.5*
Fat: *7.5 g*

Roasted Eggplant and Pepper Spread

Makes 1½ cups

1 medium eggplant, cut in half
2 T. olive oil, divided
1 green bell pepper, cored, seeded and cut in half
1 red pepper, cored, seeded and cut in half
2 T. lemon juice
1 T. tomato paste
1 T. Parmesan cheese

Preheat oven to 450°. Place the eggplant, cut side down, on an ungreased baking sheet. Roast eggplant in the oven for 15 to 20 minutes. Brush the eggplant with 1 tablespoon olive oil and add the red and green peppers to the baking sheet. Continue to roast for 25 minutes more, stopping halfway through to brush all vegetables with the remaining olive oil. Remove from oven and let vegetables cool. Peel the eggplant and drain peppers on a paper towel. Cube eggplant and chop peppers. Place in a blender or food processor and blend until well combined. Add the lemon juice, tomato paste and Parmesan cheese to the blender or food processor; blend until well combined. Refrigerate for 1 hour before serving with fresh vegetables or other low-calorie dippers.

Serving size: *¼ cup*
Calories: *56*
Fat: *3 g*

Basic Black
Bean Hummus

Makes 1½ cups

1 (15 oz.) can black beans, rinsed and drained
1 T. tahini*
1 T. low fat sour cream
4 garlic cloves, minced
1 T. minced tomato
1 T. lime juice
1 tsp. cumin
Pepper to taste

In a blender or food processor, combine black beans, tahini, sour cream, garlic cloves, tomato, lime juice, cumin and pepper. Process until smooth. Serve with fresh vegetables or baked pita chips for dipping. See page 37 for pita chip recipe.

Serving size: *2 tablespoons*
Calories: *43*
Fat: *1 g*

*Tahini, or sesame paste, is a common ingredient in hummus and other Middle Eastern and East Asian foods. It is sold fresh or dehydrated. Peanut butter can be used as a substitute for tahini, however doing so could alter the calorie and fat content. Tahini may also be omitted from the recipe.

Smoked Salmon Spread

Makes 2 to 2½ cups

1 (15 oz.) can salmon, drained
8 oz. light cream cheese, softened
¼ C. low-fat sour cream
2 T. minced onion
1 garlic clove, minced
1 T. minced parsley
½ tsp. liquid smoke
1 T. lemon juice
1 to 1½ tsp. horseradish

In a food processor or blender, combine salmon, cream cheese, sour cream, onion, garlic, parsley, liquid smoke, lemon juice and horseradish. Process until well blended. Chill in the refrigerator for 1 hour before serving. Serve with fresh vegetables, pita chips or other low-calorie crackers for dipping. See page 37 for pita chip recipe.

Serving size: *3 tablespoons*
Calories: *91*
Fat: *6 g*

Seasoned Pita Chips

Makes 48 chips

2 tsp. Italian seasoning
2 tsp. paprika
1 tsp. garlic powder
4 (6″) pita breads, cut in half

Preheat oven to 350°. In a small bowl, combine the Italian seasoning, paprika and garlic powder; set aside. Cut each pita half into six wedges. Place on an ungreased baking sheet and spray both sides of each wedge with nonstick cooking spray. Sprinkle seasoning mixture over wedges. Bake in the oven for 10 to 12 minutes or until golden brown, turning wedges over halfway through baking. Cool on wire racks before serving.

Serving size: *3 pita chips*
Calories: *43*
Fat: *trace fat*

Seasoned Eggplant Dip

Makes 2 cups

2 medium eggplants, halved lengthwise
2 T. vegetable oil, divided
1 T. minced garlic
1 tsp. ground cumin
1 T. grated fresh ginger
¼ C. minced red bell pepper
¼ C. chopped parsley
Salt and pepper to taste

Preheat oven to 400°. Line a baking sheet with foil and set aside. Brush the cut sides of the eggplant with 1 tablespoon oil and lay cut side down on the prepared baking sheet. Bake in the oven for 25 minutes or until cut sides are browned and eggplant is soft. In a medium skillet, combine remaining oil and garlic; warm until garlic sizzles over low heat. Stir in cumin and remove from heat. Peel the eggplant, finely chop and add to skillet. Return to heat and add ginger, red bell pepper and parsley. Stir mixture over low heat until blended; sprinkle with salt and pepper. Serve dip warm or at room temperature with baked pita chips, baked tortilla chips or other low-calorie crackers for dipping. See page 37 for pita chip recipe and page 31 for tortilla chip recipe.

Serving size: ¼ cup
Calories: 71
Fat: 4 g

Italian Pita Strips

Makes 48 strips

2 T. grated Parmesan cheese
½ tsp. Italian seasoning
¼ tsp. garlic powder
¼ tsp. dried rosemary, crushed
4 (6″) pita breads
2 T. butter, melted

Preheat broiler to low. Spray a baking sheet or broiling pan with nonstick cooking spray and set aside. In a small bowl, combine the Parmesan cheese, Italian seasoning, garlic powder and rosemary. Split each pita bread in half and cut into six strips about 1″ in width. Brush or spray the crust side of the pita strips with nonstick cooking spray. Place strips, crust side up, on the prepared baking sheet or broiler pan. Broil 3 to 4″ from the heat for 1 minute. Turn strips over; brush with butter and sprinkle with cheese mixture. Broil 1 to 2 minutes more or until crisp and golden.

Serving size: *5 strips*
Calories: *95*
Fat: *3.33 g*

Fabulous French Fries

2 large potatoes
1 T. olive oil
½ tsp. salt
⅛ tsp. paprika

Preheat oven to 450°. Peel potatoes and cut into slices about 4″ long and ¼″ wide. Dip fries in a bowl filled with water and ice to help potatoes crisp during baking. Remove from water and pat dry. Spread fries over an ungreased baking sheet and brush with oil. Bake in the oven for 30 to 40 minutes, turning frequently, until golden and crisp. Remove fries from oven and place on paper towels to cool. Sprinkle with salt and paprika. Serve with ketchup or low-calorie ranch dressing. See page 33 for ranch dressing recipe.

Serving size: *3 French fries*
Calories: *93*
Fat: *3 g*

Tangy Chicken Strips

Makes 24 strips

4 boneless skinless chicken breast halves
2 T. plain nonfat yogurt
15 soda crackers, crushed
1 tsp. dried thyme
½ tsp. dried marjoram
¼ tsp. curry powder
Salt to taste

Preheat oven to 375°. Trim fat from chicken and cut each breast into six strips. Coat each piece with yogurt. In shallow dish or bowl, combine cracker crumbs, thyme, marjoram, curry and salt. Roll and coat each chicken strip in the crumb mixture. Place chicken strips on an oven-proof wire rack set on a baking sheet. Bake in the oven for 25 minutes or until lightly browned and crisp. Remove from oven and let cool slightly. Serve with ketchup or low-calorie ranch dressing. See page 33 for ranch dressing recipe.

Serving size: *3 strips*
Calories: *79.5*
Fat: *1.5 g*

Cottage Cheese Dip

Makes ½ cup

⅓ C. low fat cottage cheese
2 T. shredded Cheddar cheese
¼ tsp. dillweed
⅛ tsp. salt
¼ tsp. onion powder

Place the cottage cheese in a medium bowl; mash with a fork. Add Cheddar cheese, dillweed, salt and onion powder. Stir until well combined. Serve dip with fresh vegetables or low-calorie crackers for dipping.

Serving size: *2 tablespoons*
Calories: *75*
Fat: *5 g*

Feel the Burn!

Don't sit down while waiting at the doctor's office, pharmacy or airport. Standing burns 36 more calories per hour than sitting.

Citrus Cantaloupe Salsa

Makes 12 cups

3 whole cantaloupes
4½ C. finely chopped red bell pepper
1½ C. finely chopped cilantro or parsley
1 C. finely chopped scallions
Juice of 6 limes
Pinch of salt
Pinch of red pepper flakes

Remove seeds and rind from cantaloupe and dice flesh into small pieces. In a large bowl, combine cantaloupe, red bell pepper, cilantro or parsley, scallions and lime juice. Stir until well combined. Add salt and pepper flakes. Refrigerate for 1 to 2 hours before serving with baked tortilla chips. See page 31 for tortilla chip recipe.

Serving size: ½ cup
Calories: 21
Fat: 1 g

Toasted Sesame Seed Dip

Makes ½ cup

¼ C. white sesame seeds
¼ C. black sesame seeds
1 T. kosher salt

In a large skillet over medium heat, combine white and black sesame seeds. Cook for 8 minutes, stirring often, or until white seeds have lightly browned. Transfer to a serving bowl and stir in kosher salt. Serve with fresh vegetables for dipping, such as carrot sticks, celery sticks and bell pepper strips. In order for the seeds to stick to the vegetables, you may need to spritz vegetables with water to dampen them before serving.

Serving size: *1 tablespoon*
Calories: *45*
Fat: *6 g*

Fruits & Vegetables

Juicy Jigglers

Makes 8 jigglers

2 C. apricot nectar*
3 (3 oz.) pkgs. sugar-free raspberry gelatin

In a small saucepan over medium-high heat, bring nectar to a boil. Meanwhile, pour gelatin into a small bowl. Pour hot nectar over gelatin; stir to dissolve. Pour mixture into an 8″ square pan and refrigerate for 2 hours or until firm. Cut into eight small squares.

Serving size: *2 jigglers*
Calories: *70*
Fat: *0 g*

Apricot nectar or apricot juice may not be common in your local grocery store but can be found at some organic markets. Some brands include Santa Cruz Organic Apricot Nectar and R.W. Knudsen Apricot Nectar.

Broiled Grapefruit

2 large red grapefruit
2 T. maple syrup

Preheat broiler to low. Cut each grapefruit in half and remove seeds. Cut between fruit sections for easy removal when eating. Place halves on a baking sheet and broil for 6 to 8 minutes or until tops start to brown. Remove from oven and drizzle maple syrup over grapefruit before serving.

Serving size: *1 grapefruit half*
Calories: *63*
Fat: *0 g*

Feel the Burn!

Need to do some redecorating? Painting a room for 20 minutes will burn approximately 100 calories.

Stuffed Polynesian Pears

3 oz. nonfat cream cheese, softened
1 T. powdered sugar
¼ tsp. curry powder
¼ C. flaked coconut
2 T. chopped pecans
4 ripe pears
2 T. lemon juice

In a small bowl, combine cream cheese, powdered sugar, curry powder, coconut and pecans in a small bowl. Cut each pear in half; remove and discard the stem and core. Brush cut side of pear halves with lemon juice to prevent browning. Stuff the hollow center of the pears with cheese mixture. Serve immediately or chill up to 4 hours.

Serving size: *1 pear half*
Calories: *99*
Fat: *3 g*

Bubbly Fruit Cups

Makes 3½ to 4 cups

½ C. chopped oranges
½ C. sliced bananas
½ C. chopped apples
½ C. sliced strawberries
2 T. raisins
1 (12 oz.) can sugar-free lemon-lime soda

In a medium bowl, mix oranges, bananas, apples, strawberries and raisins. Spoon into four separate cups. Pour soda over fruit and serve with a spoon.

Serving size: *1 cup*
Calories: *82*
Fat: *trace fat*

Feel the Burn!

You'll burn 50 more calories every half hour if you rake your leaves rather than use a leaf blower.

Veggie Pizza Squares

Makes 24 squares

1 (8 oz.) tube crescent rolls
3 oz. fat-free cream cheese, softened
½ C. reduced-fat buttermilk ranch salad dressing
4 C. assorted raw vegetables, cut in ½" pieces
  (cauliflower, green and red pepper, carrots
  and broccoli are recommended)
Chopped fresh chives, optional

Preheat oven to 375°. Unroll crescent rolls into a jelly roll pan sprayed with nonstick cooking spray. Press and pat rolls to seal perforations and form a crust. Bake in the oven for 8 to 10 minutes or until lightly browned. Let crust cool for 20 minutes. Meanwhile, in a medium bowl combine cream cheese and salad dressing; spread over cooled crust. Sprinkle chopped vegetables over cream cheese mixture. Cut into 24 squares to serve. Garnish with chopped chives if desired.

Serving size: 1 piece
Calories: 52
Fat: 2 g

Pineapple Almond Stuffed Celery

Makes 24 celery pieces

8 ribs celery
3 oz. nonfat cream cheese, softened
2 T. chopped almonds
2 T. crushed pineapple, drained
¼ tsp. seasoned salt
2 tsp. finely grated onion

Wash celery thoroughly and pat dry. Remove leaves and reserve for later. In a small bowl, combine cream cheese, almonds, pineapple, salt and onion; mix well. Stuff celery ribs with cream cheese mixture and cut each rib into three pieces. To serve, arrange celery pieces over a bed of the reserved celery leaves.

Serving size: *3 celery pieces*
Calories: *35*
Fat: *2 g*

Zucchini Pizza Pieces

Makes 36 pieces

3 medium zucchini, each sliced into 12 round pieces
1 (6 oz.) can tomato paste
36 thin, 1½″ square slices part skim mozzarella cheese
⅓ C. grated Parmesan cheese
Mixed Italian herbs, crumbled

Preheat broiler to low. In a medium saucepan over medium heat, parboil zucchini pieces in water for 1 minute or until tender-crisp. Remove from water with a slotted spoon and drain on paper towels. Place pieces on a baking sheet in a single layer. Top each piece with 1 teaspoon tomato paste and one slice of mozzarella cheese; top with ½ teaspoon Parmesan cheese and a sprinkling of herbs. Broil 4″ from heat source for 3 minutes or until cheese is melted and pieces are heated through. Serve pizza pieces immediately.

Serving size: *3 pizza pieces*
Calories: *90*
Fat: *6 g*

No-Fry Potato Skins

Makes 24 potato skins

4 large russet potatoes
¼ C. olive oil
1 tsp. salt
½ tsp. pepper
1½ tsp. chili powder
1½ tsp. curry powder
1½ tsp. ground coriander seed

Preheat oven to 400°. Bake potatoes in oven for 1 hour. Remove from oven, but keep the oven on. Slice potatoes in half lengthwise and scoop out centers. Leave ¼″ of the flesh on the potato skins. Discard scooped flesh or save for a separate use. Cut each potato skin crosswise into three pieces. Pour olive oil into a small cup or bowl. Dip each potato skin in olive oil and place on a large baking sheet. In a small bowl, combine salt, pepper, chili powder, curry powder and ground coriander seed. Sprinkle the mixture over the potatoes. Bake in the oven for 15 minutes or until crispy and brown. Serve potatoes immediately.

Serving size: *2 potato skins*
Calories: *92*
Fat: *4.6 g*

Roasted Chick-Peas

Makes 2 cups

2 C. cooked chick-peas, drained and rinsed
1 T. olive oil
Coarse salt

Preheat oven to 375°. In a medium bowl, toss together chick-peas and olive oil until well coated. Spread chick-peas on a baking sheet. Bake in the oven for 40 minutes or until peas are brown. Remove from oven and sprinkle with salt. Let cool before transferring to a bowl to serve.

Serving size: *¼ cup*
Calories: *29*
Fat: *0.8 g*

Feel the Burn!

FORE! One hour and 10 minutes of golfing without the use of a cart will burn about 500 calories.

Spicy Refrigerator Pickles

12 (2 to 3″) pickling cucumbers
2 C. water
1¾ C. white vinegar
1½ C. chopped fresh dillweed
½ C. sugar
8 cloves garlic, chopped
1½ tsp. coarse salt
1 T. pickling spice
1½ tsp. dill seed
½ tsp. red pepper flakes, or to taste
4 sprigs dillweed

In a large bowl, combine cucumbers, water, vinegar, chopped dillweed, sugar, garlic, salt, pickling spice, dill seed and red pepper flakes. Stir until well combined. Let stand at room temperature for 2 hours or until sugar and salt have dissolved. Place four cucumbers each into three 1½-pint wide-mouth jars. Using a ladle, transfer liquid from bowl and use to cover cucumbers in each jar. Place a sprig of dill weed in each jar and seal tightly with lids. Refrigerate for 10 days before serving. Pickles store up to one month in the refrigerator.

Serving size: 1 pickle
Calories: 66
Fat: 0.4 g

Crabby Celery Sticks

Makes 24 celery pieces

8 ribs celery
1 (6 oz.) can crab meat, drained and flaked
½ C. reduced-fat mayonnaise
2 T. ketchup
1 tsp. horseradish
1 T. pickle relish
3 drops Tabasco sauce

Wash celery thoroughly and pat dry. Remove leaves and reserve for later. In a medium bowl, combine crab meat, mayonnaise, ketchup, horseradish, pickle relish and Tabasco sauce. Stuff celery ribs with crab mixture and cut each rib into three pieces. To serve, arrange celery pieces over a bed of the reserved celery leaves.

Serving size: *3 celery pieces*
Calories: *38*
Fat: *4 g*

Citrus Fennel
and Garlic Olives

Makes 7 cups

2 T. extra-virgin olive oil

4 tsp. fennel seeds, crushed

2 garlic cloves, minced

2 lbs. assorted unpitted olives, drained (Kalamata, Italian oil-cured, Nicoise or large green are recommended)

1 tsp. freshly grated orange peel

3 (3 x 1″) strips orange peel

In a microwave-safe cup or small bowl, combine oil, fennel seeds and garlic. Heat in the microwave on high for 40 to 60 seconds. In a large bowl, toss together olives with oil mixture, orange peel and orange peel strips. Cover bowl tightly and refrigerate for at least 24 hours before serving; stir occasionally. Olives store up to one month in the refrigerator.

Serving size: *¼ cup*
Calories: *40*
Fat: *4 g*

Poblano Corn Wedges

Makes 32 wedges

2 poblano chiles or 1 red or green bell pepper
2 ears corn, husk and silk removed
2 tsp. vegetable oil
4 green onions, thinly sliced
¼ tsp. ground cumin
¼ tsp. salt
¼ tsp. pepper
2 T. chopped fresh cilantro
8 (6 to 7") flour tortillas
1 C. shredded Monterey Jack cheese

Preheat the broiler to low. Line a broiler pan with foil and set aside. Cut chiles in half lengthwise; remove and discard stem and seeds. Arrange chiles, cut side down, on the prepared pan. Broil 5 to 6" from heat for 8 to 10 minutes or until skin is charred. Remove from oven and wrap chiles in foil. Allow to steam at room temperature for 15 minutes or until cool enough to touch. Remove from foil. Peel and discard skin from chiles; finely chop. Cut corn from cobs. In a medium skillet over medium heat, warm oil. Add corn, green onions, cumin, salt and pepper. Cook for 4 to 5 minutes or until corn is tender-crisp; stir often. Remove skillet from heat and stir in chiles and cilantro. Spread mixture over four tortillas and sprinkle with cheese. Top with remaining four tortillas to make quesadillas. In a medium skillet over medium heat, cook each quesadilla for 1½ to 2 minutes per side or until cheese has melted and tortilla is browned. Cut each quesadilla into 8 wedges; serve wedges hot.

Serving size: *2 wedges*
Calories: *98*
Fat: *4 g*

Guacamole
Stuffed Celery

Makes 24 celery pieces

8 ribs celery
1 ripe avocado, peeled and mashed with a fork
2 tsp. lemon juice
¼ tsp. season salt
¼ tsp. garlic powder
¼ tsp. white pepper
¼ C. reduced-fat mayonnaise

Wash celery thoroughly and pat dry. Remove leaves and reserve for later. In a medium bowl, combine avocado, lemon juice, salt, garlic powder, white pepper and mayonnaise; mix well. Stuff celery ribs with guacamole mixture and cut each rib into three pieces. To serve, arrange celery pieces over a bed of the reserved celery leaves.

Serving size: *3 celery pieces*
Calories: *52*
Fat: *3 g*

Feel the Burn!

Chewing gum burns almost 11 calories per hour. Just make sure it's sugarless gum!

Mozzarella and Parmesan Artichokes

Makes 32 artichoke pieces

1 (14 oz.) can artichokes (8 artichokes)
½ C. reduced-calorie mayonnaise
½ C. shredded part skim mozzarella cheese
1 T. grated Parmesan cheese
Paprika
Chopped parsley

Preheat oven to 325°. Drain artichokes and pat dry with a paper towel. Cut each artichoke into four pieces. Arrange pieces in an 8″ round baking dish. In a medium bowl, combine mayonnaise, mozzarella cheese and Parmesan cheese. Spread mixture over artichoke pieces. Sprinkle paprika over top. Bake in the oven for 15 to 18 minutes or until edges are brown. Sprinkle chopped parsley over top. Serve artichoke pieces speared on toothpicks.

Serving size: *2 artichoke pieces*
Calories: *80*
Fat: *6 g*

Prosciutto Asparagus Wraps

Makes 24 wraps

24 medium asparagus spears, trimmed
12 thin slices prosciutto, cut in half lengthwise
½ C. grated Parmesan cheese

Preheat oven to 400°. In a large roasting pan, place asparagus in ¼ cup boiling water; cover. Roast in the oven for 10 to 15 minutes or until tender-crisp. Remove from oven and transfer asparagus to paper towels to drain. Wipe roasting pan dry. Place one piece of prosciutto on waxed paper; sprinkle with 1 teaspoon of Parmesan cheese. Roll one asparagus spear in the prosciutto. Repeat procedure with remaining asparagus, prosciutto and Parmesan cheese. Return wrapped spears to roasting pan and roast in oven for 10 minutes or until prosciutto begins to brown. Serve wraps warm.

Serving size: *4 wraps*
Calories: *100*
Fat: *4 g*

Grilled Peppers and Cheese

Makes 12 servings

3 large red bell peppers
⅛ tsp. salt
6 slices (¼″ thick) fresh mozzarella cheese
2 tsp. extra-virgin olive oil
1 T. chopped fresh basil leaves

Preheat grill to medium-high heat. Place bell peppers on grill; cover and cook for 10 to 13 minutes, turning every 3 to 4 minutes, until all sides are charred. Transfer peppers to a paper bag and fold top over. Let peppers stand for 5 minutes. Peel skin from peppers. Cut each in half lengthwise; remove and discard stems, seeds and ribs. Sprinkle peppers with salt. Place one slice of cheese on each pepper half and drizzle with oil. Cook peppers on grill 5 minutes more or until cheese is melted. Sprinkle basil over peppers. To serve, cut each pepper in half again.

Serving size: *1 pepper piece*
Calories: *60*
Fat: *4.5 g*

Black Forest Ham Asparagus Wraps

Makes 24 wraps

24 medium asparagus spears, trimmed
12 thin slices Black Forest ham*, cut lengthwise in half
1 C. shredded Gruyère cheese

Preheat oven to 400°. In a large roasting pan, place asparagus in ¼ cup boiling water; cover. Roast in the oven for 10 to 15 minutes or until tender-crisp. Remove from oven and transfer asparagus to paper towels to drain. Wipe roasting pan dry. Place one piece of ham on waxed paper; sprinkle with 1 teaspoon of Gruyère cheese. Roll one spear of asparagus in the ham. Repeat procedure with remaining asparagus, ham and Gruyère cheese. Return wrapped spears to roasting pan and roast in oven for 10 minutes or until ham begins to brown. Serve wraps warm.

Serving size: *2 wraps*
Calories: *80*
Fat: *6 g*

*Black Forest ham is a variety of smoked ham produced in the Black Forest region of Germany. The production of Black Forest ham can take up to three months. Raw ham is salted and seasoned with garlic, coriander, pepper, juniper berries and other spices. After curing for two weeks, the salt is removed and the ham cures for two weeks more. The ham is then smoked for several weeks. During this period it becomes very red in color. The smoke is created by burning fir brush and sawdust. The smoking process gives the ham much of its flavor. The term, "Black Forest ham", is a protected designation of origin in the European Union (EU). Anything sold in the EU as "Black Forest ham" must come from the Black Forest regions of Germany. However, this is not the case in non-EU countries, particularly the United States and Canada; as a result, most of the "Black Forest ham" sold in the non-EU countries bears little or no resemblance to the German product.

Savory Stuffed Mushrooms

Makes 24 mushrooms

24 fresh mushrooms
1 carrot, grated
3 oz. fat-free cream cheese, softened
2 T. fresh chopped chives or 1 tsp. dried chives
1 T. grated fresh onion or 1 tsp. dried minced onion

Preheat broiler to low. Remove stems and wipe off mushroom caps. Discard stems or reserve for a separate use. In a medium bowl, combine cream cheese, chives and onion; mix well. Stuff a portion of the mixture into each mushroom cap. Place mushroom caps on an ungreased baking sheet. Broil for 8 minutes. Serve mushrooms hot.

Serving size: *6 mushrooms*
Calories: *54*
Fat: *0 g*

Zucchini Tuna Bites

Makes 8 bites

¼ tsp. Worcestershire sauce
1 tsp. lemon juice
¼ tsp. garlic powder
2 tsp. dried parsley flakes
2 tsp. reduced-calorie mayonnaise
2 tsp. fat-free yogurt
⅓ C. water-packed tuna, well-drained
1 small zucchini, cut into eight ½″ slices
2 tsp. grated Parmesan cheese

In a small bowl, combine Worcestershire sauce, lemon juice, garlic powder, parsley, mayonnaise and yogurt; mix well. Stir in tuna. Spread 2 teaspoons of the tuna mixture onto each zucchini slice. Sprinkle ¼ teaspoon of Parmesan cheese over each bite before serving.

Serving size: *4 zucchini bites*
Calories: *98*
Fat: *2 g*

Salsa Veggie Roll-Ups

Makes 24 roll-ups

1 (3 oz.) pkg. cream cheese, softened

⅓ C. sour cream

1 T. taco seasoning mix

½ C. fresh corn kernels or Green Giant® Niblets®
  frozen corn, thawed, drained

½ C. black beans (from 15 oz. can), drained, rinsed

¼ C. finely chopped fresh cilantro

1 Roma tomato, seeded, finely chopped

2 T. chunky salsa

3 (10˝) garden spinach and vegetable, tomato
  or plain flour tortillas (10˝)

In small bowl, beat together cream cheese, sour cream and taco seasoning mix until well combined. Stir in corn, beans, cilantro, tomato and salsa. Spread cream cheese mixture over each tortilla. Roll up the tortillas and cut off tapered ends. Wrap each tortilla in plastic wrap; refrigerate at least 1 hour but no longer than 8 hours before serving. Cut each roll into 1˝ slices to serve.

Serving size: *1 roll-up*
Calories: *60*
Fat: *2.5 g*

Feeling
Fancy

Devilishly Delicious Eggs

Makes 24 deviled eggs

12 large eggs
½ C. fresh breadcrumbs
¼ C. reduced-fat sour cream
2 T. chives or scallions, chopped
1 T. Dijon mustard
Salt to taste
Pepper to taste
1 tsp. paprika, optional

Using a spoon, lightly tap each egg to make a hairline crack. Place eggs in a large saucepan and cover with cold water. Bring water to a simmer over medium heat; simmer eggs for 9 minutes. Drain water from saucepan and set the pan and eggs under cold running water for 1 to 2 minutes. Drain water from pan again; shake eggs in pan to crack and loosen shells. Peel eggs and slice in half lengthwise. Scoop the yolks out of the eggs. Only half the yolks are needed for this recipe, so discard half the yolks for a separate use. Set all egg whites aside. In a small bowl, mash the egg yolks. Mix in breadcrumbs, sour cream, chives or scallions and mustard. Season with salt and pepper. Spoon yolk mixture into hollow egg whites and sprinkle paprika over top if desired.

Serving size: *2 deviled eggs*
Calories: *90*
Fat: *6 g*

Spinach-Stuffed Mushrooms

Makes 12 mushrooms

12 large white mushrooms, about 1½″ across
1 tsp. vegetable oil
¾ C. minced onion
½ tsp. minced garlic
½ C. finely chopped spinach
½ C. seeded and chopped red or green bell peppers
1 T. fresh thyme
¼ tsp. salt
Pinch of pepper
1 T. grated Parmesan cheese

Preheat broiler to low. Remove mushroom stems and finely chop; set aside. Bring a medium pot of water to a boil. Blanch mushroom caps for 2 minutes. Remove caps from water and place, gill side down, on a paper towel to drain. Coat a medium skillet with nonstick cooking spray; add the vegetable oil and heat. When hot, add chopped mushroom stems, onions, garlic, spinach, peppers, thyme, salt and pepper; cook for 6 minutes, stirring periodically. Remove skillet from heat and let cool. Spoon the mixture into the mushroom caps and place stuffed mushrooms on a baking sheet. Sprinkle Parmesan cheese over the mushrooms; broil mushrooms for 3 minutes or until slightly brown. Let cool slightly before serving.

Serving size: *6 mushrooms*
Calories: *90*
Fat: *6 g*

Veggie Kabobs

Makes 6 kabobs

12 oz. white mushrooms

10 large scallions

2 red or green bell peppers, seeded and cut
 into 1½" squares

¼ C. reduced-sodium soy sauce

2 T. sugar

1 T. sesame oil

4 tsp. minced garlic

2 T. sesame seeds, toasted*, divided

½ tsp. pepper

Trim and discard stems from mushroom caps. Cut caps into ½" thick slices. Trim off the white parts of the scallions and slice into 1½" pieces; set aside. Trim and chop enough of the scallion greens to make ¼ cup; set aside. Alternate threading mushroom slices, scallion slices and pepper squares onto six separate skewers. Place kabobs snuggly in a baking dish; set aside. In a small bowl, whisk together soy sauce, sugar, oil, garlic, 1 tablespoon sesame seeds and pepper. Pour marinade over kabobs, coating all sides. Cover and place in refrigerator to marinate for up to 2 hours. Turn kabobs once while marinating. Preheat grill to high. Cook kabobs on the grill for 3 to 5 minutes on each side. Brush often with any remaining marinade. Remove from grill and sprinkle remaining sesame seeds and scallion greens over kabobs before serving. Leftover marinade may be used for dipping.

Serving size: *1 kabob*
Calories: *90*
Fat: *4 g*

*To toast, place sesame seeds in a single layer on a baking sheet. Bake at 350° for approximately 8 minutes or until sesame seeds are golden brown.

Tasty Tomato
Ricotta Bruschetta

Makes 16 bruschetta slices

1 (8 oz.) loaf Italian bread, cut diagonally into
   ½″ thick pieces

1 clove garlic, peeled and cut in half

6 medium plum tomatoes, seeded and cut into
   ½″ thick pieces

1 T. finely chopped red onion

1 T. chopped fresh basil

4 oz. ricotta salata*

2 T. extra-virgin olive oil

2 tsp. balsamic vinegar

¼ tsp. salt

¼ tsp. black pepper

Preheat oven to 400°. Place Italian bread slices on an ungreased baking sheet. Bake in the oven for 5 minutes or until lightly toasted. Remove from oven and rub one side of each slice with cut side of garlic. In a small bowl, toss together tomatoes, onion, basil, ricotta salata, oil, vinegar, salt and pepper until well combined. To serve, spoon mixture onto garlic-rubbed side of bread.

Serving size: *1 bruschetta slice*
Calories: *79*
Fat: *4 g*

*Ricotta salata is an Italian sheep's milk cheese. The milk curds and whey used to make this cheese are pressed and dried even before the cheese is aged, giving the pure white cheese a dense but slightly spongy texture and a salty, milky flavor. If you are unable to find Ricotta Salata, Feta cheese may be substituted.

Rich Ribbon
Tea Sandwiches

1 (8 oz.) pkg. cream cheese, softened
2 small green onions, finely chopped
4 radishes, finely chopped
3 T. chopped fresh parsley
⅛ tsp. salt
⅛ tsp. pepper
18 thin slices whole wheat bread
12 thin slices white bread

Line a jelly roll pan with dampened paper towels. In a small bowl, mix cream cheese, green onions, radishes, parsley, salt and pepper until well blended. To create one sandwich stack, spread cream cheese mixture on two slices wheat bread and two slices white bread. Starting with wheat, stack the slices alternating bread types with cream cheese mixture facing up. Top the stack with a plain piece of wheat bread. Repeat with remaining bread and cheese mixture to make six stacks. Press down gently on each stack; trim off crusts using a serrated knife and place in the prepared pan. Cover with another dampened paper towel to keep sandwiches from drying out. Cover tightly and refrigerate for 3 to 4 hours. To serve, cut each stack diagonally into quarters and arrange on a serving platter.

Serving size: *1 tea sandwich*
Calories: *79*
Fat: *4 g*

White Bean Bruschetta

1 (8 oz.) loaf Italian bread, cut diagonally into
 ½˝ thick slices

1 clove garlic, peeled and cut in half

1 (15.5 oz.) can white kidney beans,
 rinsed and drained

1 T. fresh lemon juice

1 T. olive oil

3 tsp. chopped fresh parsley, divided

1 tsp. chopped fresh sage

¼ tsp. salt

⅛ tsp. pepper

Preheat oven to 400°. Place Italian bread slices on an ungreased baking sheet. Bake in the oven for 5 minutes or until lightly toasted. Remove from oven and rub one side of each slice with cut side of garlic. In a medium bowl, lightly mash kidney beans and lemon juice with a fork. Stir in olive oil, 2 teaspoons parsley, sage, salt and pepper. To serve, spoon mixture onto garlic-rubbed side of toast and sprinkle with remaining chopped parsley.

Serving size: *3 bruschetta slices*
Calories: *99*
Fat: *3 g*

Smoked Salmon Sandwiches

Makes 32 tea sandwiches

8 thin slices white bread
8 thin slices wheat bread
6 T. butter or margarine, softened
6 oz. thinly sliced smoked salmon

Line a jelly roll pan with dampened paper towels. Lightly spread once side of each bread slice with butter or margarine. Arrange salmon on buttered side of white bread and top with a slice of wheat bread. Trim crusts off and cut each sandwich diagonally into quarters. Repeat with remaining bread and salmon. Place sandwiches in prepared pan. Cover with another dampened paper towel to keep sandwiches from drying out. Cover tightly and refrigerate for 3 to 4 hours. To serve, arrange sandwiches on a serving platter.

Serving size: *2 tea sandwiches*
Calories: *86*
Fat: *6 g*

Tomato Basil Bruschetta

Makes 16 bruschetta slices

1 (8 oz.) loaf French bread, cut diagonally into
  ½˝ thick slices
1 clove garlic, peeled and cut in half
8 small tomatoes, chopped
¼ C. Kalamata olives, pitted and chopped
¼ C. chopped fresh basil
¼ C. chopped fresh parsley
3 T. extra-virgin olive oil
¼ tsp. salt
⅛ tsp. pepper

Preheat oven to 400°. Place French bread slices on an ungreased baking sheet. Bake in the oven for 5 minutes or until lightly toasted. Remove from oven and rub one side of each slice with cut side of garlic. In a medium bowl, toss together tomatoes, olives, basil, parsley, oil, salt and pepper. To serve, spoon mixture onto garlic-rubbed side of toast.

Serving size: *1 bruschetta slice*
Calories: *70*
Fat: *4 g*

Crab-Stuffed Cherry Tomatoes

Makes 36 tomatoes

36 cherry tomatoes
1 tsp. salt
¼ C. low-fat cottage cheese
1½ tsp. minced onion
½ tsp. horseradish, drained
1½ tsp. fresh lemon juice
⅛ tsp. garlic powder
½ lb. crab meat, drained and flaked
½ C. minced celery
1 T. finely chopped green bell pepper
Pinch of parsley

Cut off tops of tomatoes and remove pulp. Sprinkle insides of tomatoes with salt. Invert tomatoes and let drain on a paper towel. Meanwhile, using a food processor or blender, process the cottage cheese until smooth. Add onion, horseradish, lemon juice and garlic powder; process 1 minute more. Transfer to a medium bowl and stir in crab meat, celery and green pepper. Stuff each hollowed tomato with crabmeat filling. Refrigerate for 1 hour. To serve, arrange tomatoes on a serving platter and garnish each tomato with parsley.

Serving size: *6 tomatoes*
Calories: *70*
Fat: *trace fat*

Cucumber Mint Sandwiches

Makes 32 tea sandwiches

1 seedless cucumber
½ tsp. salt
5 T. butter or margarine, softened
16 thin slices white or wheat bread
32 fresh mint leaves

Line a jelly roll pan with dampened paper towels. Cut cucumber in half lengthwise and across into paper thin slices. Set a colander over a bowl and toss together cucumber and salt. Cover and refrigerate for 30 minutes, stirring periodically. Drain liquid from bowl and pat cucumber slices dry with paper towels. Spread butter on each slice of bread. Arrange cucumber on eight buttered bread slices and place one mint leaf in each corner of each slice. Top with remaining unbuttered bread slices. Trim crusts off and cut each sandwich diagonally into quarters. Place sandwiches in prepared pan. Cover with another dampened paper towel to keep sandwiches from drying out. Cover tightly and refrigerate for 3 to 4 hours. To serve, arrange sandwiches on a serving platter.

Serving size: *2 tea sandwiches*
Calories: *72*
Fat: *2 g*

Mango Basil Bruschetta

Makes 32 bruschetta slices

1 (1 lb.) loaf French bread, cut into ½" pieces
1 mango, peeled, seeded and diced
1 T. fresh basil, minced
1 C. grated Romano cheese

Preheat broiler to low. Place French bread slices on an ungreased baking sheet. Broil for 1 to 2 minutes on each side or until lightly toasted. In a medium bowl, combine mango and fresh basil. Spoon mixture onto each slice of bread. Sprinkle Romano cheese over top. Return to oven and broil 2 to 3 minutes more or until the cheese is melted and lightly browned. Serve bruschetta warm.

Serving size: *1 bruschetta slice*
Calories: *57*
Fat: *1.5 g*

Feel the Burn!

Make your bed, not just to keep the house clean, but to burn about 17 calories, too.

Fresh Strawberry Bruschetta

1½ (8 oz.) loaves French bread, cut into ½″ slices
1 T. butter, softened
2 C. chopped fresh strawberries
¼ C. sugar

Preheat broiler to low. Spread a thin layer of butter on each bread slice. Arrange bread slices in a single layer on an ungreased baking sheet. Broil for 1 to 2 minutes on each side or until lightly toasted. Spoon a portion of chopped strawberries onto each piece of toast. Sprinkle sugar over the strawberries. Return to oven and broil 2 to 3 minutes more or until sugar is caramelized. Serve bruschetta warm.

Serving size: *1 bruschetta slice*
Calories: *57.5*
Fat: *1 g*

Grilled Salmon Kabobs

Makes 12 kabobs

1 lb. skinless salmon filet
¼ C. soy sauce
¼ C. honey
1 T. rice vinegar
1 tsp. minced fresh gingerroot
1 clove garlic, minced
Pinch of pepper
12 fresh lemon wedges

Slice salmon lengthwise into 12 strips. Thread each slice onto a soaked wooden skewer and place in a shallow dish. In a medium bowl, whisk together the soy sauce, honey, vinegar, gingerroot, garlic and pepper. Pour mixture over kabobs, turning to coat. Let kabobs marinate at room temperature for 30 minutes. Transfer marinade to a small saucepan and simmer over low heat for several minutes. Preheat the grill to medium-high heat and lightly oil the grate. Thread one lemon wedge onto the end of each skewer. Grill kabobs for 3 to 4 minutes per side or until fish flakes easily with a fork; brush often with marinade. Let cool slightly before serving. Discard any remaining marinade.

Serving size: *1 kabob*
Calories: *89*
Fat: *3.7 g*

Fennel Brushed Grilled Oysters

Makes 24 oysters

1 C. butter, softened
1 tsp. fennel seed, ground
1 T. minced shallots
1 T. chopped fennel greens
1 tsp. pepper
½ tsp. salt
24 unopened, fresh, live medium oysters

Preheat the grill to medium heat. In a small bowl, combine butter, ground fennel seeds, shallots, fennel greens, pepper and salt; blend until well combined and set aside. Arrange oysters on the grill, cover and cook for 3 to 5 minutes or until oysters begin hissing and start to open. Pry each shell open at the hinge and loosen the oyster; discard the flat shell. Brush each oyster with ½ teaspoon of the fennel butter. Return to grill and cook until butter is melted and hot. Let cool slightly before serving.

Serving size: *1 oyster*
Calories: *77*
Fat: *7.8 g*

Blue Cheese and Roasted Portobello Mushrooms

Makes 2 mushrooms

2 portobello mushrooms, stems removed
1 T. soy sauce, or to taste
Pepper to taste
3 T. crumbled blue cheese

Preheat oven to 425°. Place mushroom caps, gill side up, on an ungreased baking sheet. Drizzle mushrooms with soy sauce and sprinkle with pepper. Bake in the oven for 25 minutes. Remove from oven, and sprinkle 1½ tablespoons blue cheese over each mushroom. Return mushrooms to oven and bake 10 minutes more or until cheese is melted. Serve mushrooms warm.

Serving size: *1 mushroom*
Calories: *79*
Fat: *3.9 g*

Cookies,
Bars &
Brownies

Chocolate Chip Cookies

Makes 50 cookies

1 C. unsalted margarine
2¼ C. all-purpose flour, divided
1 C. sugar
½ C. packed brown sugar
½ C. oat bran
2 egg whites
2 tsp. vanilla extract
½ tsp. baking soda
¼ tsp. salt
½ C. mini semi-sweet chocolate chips

Preheat oven to 375°. In a large bowl, beat the margarine with an electric mixer on medium to high speed for 30 seconds. Add 1 cup flour, sugar, brown sugar, oat bran, egg whites, vanilla extract, baking soda and salt. Beat until thoroughly combined, periodically scraping mixture from the sides of the bowl. Beat in the remaining flour. Stir in chocolate pieces. Drop by rounded teaspoonfuls onto a ungreased baking sheet about 2″ apart. Bake in the oven for 8 to 10 minutes or until cookie edges are lightly brown. Remove from oven and cool on a wire rack.

Serving size: *1 cookie*
Calories: *86*
Fat: *4 g*

Chocolate Raspberry Bars

Makes 48 bars

1½ C. flour
¾ C. sugar
¾ C. butter, softened
1 (10 oz.) pkg. frozen raspberries, thawed
¼ C. orange juice
1 T. cornstarch
¾ C. mini semi-sweet chocolate chips

Preheat oven to 350°. In a large bowl, combine flour, sugar and butter. Press the mixture into the bottom of an ungreased 9 x 13″ baking pan. Bake in the oven for 15 minutes. Meanwhile, in a 1-quart saucepan, combine the raspberries, orange juice and cornstarch. Heat to a boil; let boil and stir for 1 minute. Remove from heat and cool for 10 minutes. Sprinkle chocolate chips over the baked crust and spoon the raspberry mixture over the top. Return to the oven and bake 20 minutes more or until raspberry mixture has set. Remove from oven and cool. Cut into 1 x 2″ bars.

Serving size: *1 bar*
Calories: *74*
Fat: *3.9 g*

Festive Candy Cane Meringues

Makes 48 cookies

3 egg whites
½ tsp. cream of tartar
¾ C. sugar
¼ tsp. peppermint extract
Red paste food coloring

Preheat the oven to 225°. Line a baking sheet with parchment paper and set aside. In a medium bowl, beat the egg whites until foamy. Add the cream of tartar and, using an electric mixer, beat on medium speed until stiff peaks form. Slowly add sugar, 1 tablespoon at a time; beat for 6 minutes on high or until stiff peaks form and sugar dissolves. Beat in the peppermint extract. Cut a small hole in a pastry bag and insert a star tip. On the inside of the pastry bag, brush stripes of red food coloring spaced about ¼" apart. Brush stripes from the tip of the bag to about ¾" from the top. Carefully fill the pastry bag with meringue mixture. Pipe candy canes about 3" in size onto the prepared baking sheet. Bake in the oven for 25 minutes. Rotate baking sheet to different rack and bake 25 minutes more or until firm. Turn the oven off and leave the meringues in the oven for 1 hour more with the door ajar.

Serving size: *4 cookies*
Calories: *52*
Fat: *0 g*

Creamy Pudding Cookies

Makes 50 cookies

2 C. whipping cream
5½ T. sugar-free instant chocolate pudding mix

Line baking sheets with waxed paper and set aside. In a medium bowl, whip the cream until soft peaks form. Fold in the pudding mix. Drop the mixture by rounded teaspoonfuls onto prepared baking sheets. Freeze on baking sheets until set. Transfer cookies to large re-sealable bags to store in the freezer.

Serving size: *2 cookies*
Calories: *72*
Fat: *7.2 g*

Feel the Burn!

Do you ever feel the need to get up from your desk and move around? Jogging in place for just 12 minutes will burn a little more than 100 calories.

Low Calorie Macaroons

Makes 30 cookies

2 egg whites
½ tsp. vanilla extract
⅛ tsp. cream of tartar
⅔ C. sugar
¾ C. flaked coconut

Preheat oven to 325°. Spray a baking sheet with nonstick cooking spray and set aside. Place egg whites in a small bowl and let stand at room temperature for about 30 minutes. Add the vanilla extract and cream of tartar to the egg whites; beat with an electric mixer on medium speed until soft peaks form. Slowly add the sugar, 1 tablespoon at a time. Beat with the mixer on high speed for 7 minutes or until stiff peaks form and sugar is almost dissolved. Carefully fold in the coconut. Drop the mixture by rounded teaspoonfuls about 2″ apart on the prepared baking sheet. Bake in the oven for 12 to 15 minutes or until lightly browned. Remove from oven and let cool on wire racks.

Serving size: *3 cookies*
Calories: *78*
Fat: *3 g*

Molasses Brandy Snaps

Makes 24 cookies

½ C. butter (no substitutes)
3 T. light molasses
½ C. flour
½ C. sugar

1 tsp. ground ginger
¼ tsp. salt
2 T. brandy

Preheat oven to 350°. Grease a large baking sheet and set aside. In a 2-quart saucepan, melt the butter and molasses over medium-low heat, stirring periodically until smooth. Remove saucepan from heat. Using a wooden spoon, stir in the flour, sugar, ginger and salt until well combined and smooth, then stir in the brandy. Place saucepan in a bowl of hot water to keep warm. Drop 1 teaspoonful of batter on the prepared baking sheet. Using a small metal spatula, spread batter in a circular motion to make a 4″ circle. Repeat to make four circles placing each 2″ apart. Batter spreads during baking so do not place more than four circles on a baking sheet. Bake in the oven for 5 minutes or until golden brown. Remove from oven and cool for 30 to 60 seconds, just until edges have set. Using a wide spatula, carefully flip the cookies. As quickly as possible, roll each cookie around wooden spoon handle or dowel about ½″ in diameter. As each cookie becomes shaped, carefully slip it off the handle or dowel and place on a wire rack to cool. Repeat with the remaining batter.

Serving size: *1 cookie*
Calories: *72*
Fat: *4 g*

Tasty Tip

To satisfy your sweet tooth even more, fill your Molasses Brandy Snaps with 2 tablespoons of Lite Cool Whip. Doing so will add 20 calories and 1 gram of fat to each cookie.

Perfect Pumpkin Bars

Makes 24 bars

1 C. flour
⅔ C. sugar
1 tsp. baking powder
1 tsp. ground cinnamon
½ tsp. baking soda
⅛ tsp. salt
⅛ tsp. ground cloves

1 C. canned pumpkin
2 egg whites
¼ C. cooking oil,
  slightly beaten
¼ C. water
Cream Cheese Frosting,
  *recipe below

Preheat oven to 350°. Spray a 7 x 11″ baking pan with nonstick cooking spray and set aside. In a medium bowl, combine flour, sugar, baking powder, cinnamon, baking soda, salt and cloves. Stir in the pumpkin, egg whites, oil and water until well combined. Spread the batter into the bottom of the prepared baking pan. Bake in the oven for 20 to 25 minutes or until wooden toothpick inserted in the center comes out clean. Remove from oven and let cool in the pan. Once bars are cool, spread cream cheese frosting over top and cut into 24 squares. Cover and store in the refrigerator.

Serving size: *1 bar*
Calories: *97*
Fat: *3 g*

*Cream Cheese Frosting

In a medium bowl, combine ¼ cup light cream cheese, 1 cup sifted powdered sugar, 1 teaspoon vanilla extract and ¼ teaspoon grated lemon or orange peel. Beat until mixture is light and fluffy. Gradually beat in another ¾ cup sifted powdered sugar. Spread frosting over cooled pumpkin bars before serving.

Chocoholics
Low-Cal Brownies

Makes 24 brownies

½ C. flour
6 T. unsweetened cocoa powder
1 C. sugar
⅛ tsp. salt
2 T. vegetable oil
½ tsp. vanilla extract
1 (4 oz.) jar pureed baby food prunes
2 eggs

Preheat oven to 350°. Grease an 8″ square pan and set aside. In a medium bowl, combine flour, cocoa powder, sugar and salt. Add oil, vanilla, prunes and eggs; stir until well combined. Spread the batter evenly into the bottom of the prepared baking pan. Bake in the oven for 30 minutes or until top is shiny and a wooden toothpick inserted in the center comes out clean. Cut into 24 squares.

Serving size: *1 brownie*
Calories: *65*
Fat: *1.8 g*

Classic Cake Brownies

Makes 24 brownies

¼ C. unsalted margarine
⅔ C. sugar
¼ C. unsweetened
   cocoa powder
1 egg white
½ tsp. vanilla extract
⅓ C. skim milk
¾ C. flour

¼ tsp. baking powder
¼ tsp. baking soda
⅓ C. chopped walnuts
   or pecans
1 tsp. powdered sugar
Chocolate Drizzle
   Icing,*recipe below

Preheat oven to 350°. Spray a 9″ square baking pan with nonstick cooking spray and set aside. In a medium saucepan over medium-high heat, melt the margarine. Remove pan from heat and stir in the sugar and cocoa powder until well combined. Add egg white and vanilla extract; beat lightly with a wooden spoon until combined. Stir in the milk; add the flour, baking powder and baking soda, using the spoon to beat until well combined. Stir in the walnuts or pecans and spread the batter into the bottom of the prepared baking pan. Bake in the oven for 10 to 18 minutes or until a toothpick inserted in the center comes out clean. Remove from oven and cool in the pan. Sprinkle powdered sugar over the brownies and drizzle with chocolate icing. Let stand for 30 minutes or until icing is set. Cut into 24 squares.

Serving size: *1 brownie*
Calories: *74*
Fat: *3 g*

*Chocolate Drizzle Icing

In a small bowl, combine ½ cup sifted powdered sugar, 1 tablespoon unsweetened cocoa powder, ¼ teaspoon vanilla extract and 1 to 2 tablespoons of skim milk; mix until of desired consistency. Drizzle over cooled brownines.

Desserts

Lemon Almond Biscotti

Makes 36 biscotti

2 C. flour
¾ C. sugar
½ C. finely ground almonds
½ tsp. baking powder
½ tsp. baking soda
1 T. grated lemon peel
3 T. poppy seeds
1 egg
2 egg whites
1 tsp. lemon extract

Preheat oven to 350°. Line a baking sheet with parchment paper and set aside. In a medium bowl, combine the flour, sugar, almonds, baking powder and baking soda; set aside. In a different medium bowl, combine the lemon peel, poppy seeds, egg, egg whites and lemon extract. Add the flour mixture to the lemon and egg mixture; mix well. Divide dough in half and form two logs. Place logs on a prepared baking sheet. Bake in the oven for 30 minutes. Remove from oven and let cool slightly before cutting the logs into ½″ wide slices. Spread slices out on baking sheet and return to oven to bake 8 to 10 minutes more or until dry. Let biscotti cool completely before storing in an airtight container.

Serving size: *1 biscotti*
Calories: *60*
Fat: *1.5 g*

Berry Grilled Peaches

Makes 4 servings

4 ripe peaches
1 C. fresh or frozen raspberries
2 to 3 T. brown sugar
4 tsp. freshly squeezed lemon juice

Preheat grill to low. Wash peaches, cut in half and remove pits. Place one peach, cut side up, on a square of aluminum foil and fill the cavity with ¼ cup raspberries. Sprinkle the berries with some of the brown sugar and lemon juice. Fold the foil over the peach half so it is completely covered. Repeat entire process with remaining peach halves. Cook peaches on grill for 15 to 20 minutes. Remove from grill and let cool slightly before unwrapping peaches. Serve peaches warm.

Serving size: *2 peach halves*
Calories: *86*
Fat: *0 g*

Tasty Tip

To sweeten up your peaches, drop ½ tablespoon Lite Cool Whip on top of each peach half. Doing so will only add 10 calories and ½ gram of fat to a serving.

White Ice
Cream Truffles

Makes 6 ice cream truffles

3 C. nonfat vanilla ice cream, softened
2 oz. white chocolate, grated
½ C. black coffee, room temperature
⅓ C. coffee liqueur

Scoop and form ice cream into six balls; place balls on a baking sheet. Freeze until ice cream balls are firm. Place grated white chocolate in a shallow bowl or dish. Remove ice cream balls from freezer and quickly roll in grated chocolate. In a medium bowl, combine black coffee and liqueur. Divide mixture evenly among six bowls. Place one ice-cream ball in each bowl to serve.

Serving size: *1 ice-cream ball*
Calories: *98*
Fat: *3.1 g*

Feel the Burn!

Keep it clean! Nearly 25 minutes of vacuuming around your home will burn about 100 calories.

Vanilla
Almond Biscotti

Makes 42 biscotti

⅓ C. butter, softened
1 C. Equal Sugar Lite
2 eggs
1 tsp. vanilla extract
2¼ C. flour
½ C. almond slices, toasted*
1½ tsp. baking powder
½ tsp. salt

Preheat oven to 325°. Line a baking sheet with parchment paper and set aside. In a medium bowl, beat butter and Equal Sugar Lite until well combined. Beat in eggs and vanilla extract. In another medium bowl, combine flour, almonds, baking powder and salt until well blended. Add flour mixture to butter mixture; stir until well combined. Divide dough in half evenly and form into two logs; place on prepared baking sheet. Bake in the oven for 30 minutes. Remove from oven and let cool slightly before cutting the logs into ½″ wide slices. Spread slices out on the baking sheet and return to oven to bake 8 to 10 minutes more or until dry; turn slices over half way through baking. Let biscotti cool completely before storing in an airtight container.

Serving size: *1 biscotti*
Calories: *81*
Fat: *3 g*

*To toast, place sliced almonds in a single layer on a baking sheet. Bake at 350° for 10 minutes or until almonds are golden brown.

Chocolate Coconut Truffles

2 C. semi-sweet chocolate chips
¼ C. orange-flavored liqueur or 1 tsp. orange extract
1 (16 oz.) can chocolate frosting
½ C. flaked coconut

In a medium saucepan over low heat, melt chocolate chips stirring constantly; remove from heat. Stir in orange liqueur or orange extract and frosting; blend until well combined. Refrigerate 1 to 2 hours or until firm. Place coconut in the bottom of a pie pan or shallow bowl. Scoop chocolate mixture into 1″ balls and drop onto coconut. (Mixture will be sticky.) Roll balls to coat completely. Place each truffle in a foil candy cup and store in refrigerator.

Serving size: 1 truffle
Calories: 60
Fat: 3 g

Frozen
Treats

Cran-Raspberry Popsicles

Makes 8 popsicles

1 (12 oz.) can frozen cranberry-raspberry
   juice concentrate
2 C. water

In a large bowl or pitcher, combine cranberry-raspberry juice concentrate with water; stir until well combined. Divide mixture into eight 3-ounce plastic or paper cups. Cover each cup with a small piece of aluminum foil and poke a popsicle stick through the foil and into the cup. Freeze cups for 2 to 3 hours or until firm. To serve, remove foil and peel cup away from popsicle.

Serving size: *1 popsicle*
Calories: *66*
Fat: *0 g*

Frosty Pecan Fruit Cups

Makes 12 fruit cups

2 C. nonfat orange and pineapple yogurt
1 (17 oz.) can apricot halves, drained and cut up
¼ C. chopped pecans

In a large bowl, combine yogurt and apricots. Divide and spoon mixture into 12 paper-lined muffin cups. Sprinkle pecans over the top. Cover and freeze for 2 hours or until firm. Remove from freezer and peel paper off frozen fruit cups. Serve in small bowls or fruit dishes. Cups freeze up to one month.

Serving size: *1 fruit cup*
Calories: *74*
Fat: *3 g*

Feel the Burn!

You'll burn an extra 280 calories an hour if you wash your car yourself rather than cruising through the automatic car wash.

Bananasicles

1 (3.4 oz.) pkg. instant banana pudding mix
2 C. skim milk
1 banana, cut into pieces

In a large bowl, combine instant pudding mix and milk until thick. Stir in banana chunks; mix until well combined. Divide and spoon mixture into seven 3-ounce plastic or paper cups. Cover each cup with a small piece of aluminum foil and poke a popsicle stick through the foil and into the cup. Freeze cups for 2 to 3 hours or until firm, tapping periodically to remove bubbles. To serve, remove foil and peel cup away from popsicle.

Serving size: 1 popsicle
Calories: 75
Fat: 5 g

Frozen Fruit and Cream Cups

¼ C. walnuts
2 ripe bananas
2 C. fat-free sour cream
1 (8 oz.) can unsweetened crushed pineapple
⅓ C. mini marshmallows
¼ C. sugar
1 tsp. vanilla extract

Place walnuts in a blender and pulse until chopped. Add bananas and continue to pulse until blended. Add sour cream, pineapple, marshmallows, sugar and vanilla extract; pulse until blended. Spoon ¼ cup of the mixture into 12 paper-lined muffin cups. Freeze for 2 hours or until firm. Remove from freezer and peel paper off frozen fruit cups. Serve in small bowls or fruit dishes.

Serving size: *1 fruit cup*
Calories: *94*
Fat: *2 g*

Lemon Sorbet

1 C. sugar
3 C. water
1 tsp. finely shredded lemon peel
½ C. fresh lemon juice
2 to 3 drops yellow food coloring

In a medium saucepan over medium heat, bring sugar and water to a boil. Remove from heat and let cool thoroughly. Cover and refrigerate until chilled. In a 9″ square baking pan, combine chilled syrup mixture, lemon peel and lemon juice; mix well. Add food coloring; cover and freeze for 3 to 4 hours or until almost firm. Remove from freezer and break frozen mixture into chunks; transfer to a chilled bowl. Using an electric mixer, beat on medium speed until fluffy but not melted. Transfer sorbet to a 4- to 6-cup container with a lid; cover and freeze until firm. To serve, let stand at room temperature for 5 minutes before scooping into small bowls.

Serving size: *½ cup*
Calories: *89*
Fat: *0 g*

Honey-Banana Yogurt Popsicles

Makes 6 popsicles

1 banana, sliced
1 C. plain low-fat yogurt
3 T. honey

Using a food processor or blender, combine banana chunks, yogurt and honey; blend until smooth. Transfer to a bowl, cover and freeze until mushy. Remove from freezer and, using an electric mixer, beat on medium speed until mixture is of pourable consistency. Divide and pour mixture into six 3-ounce plastic or paper cups. Cover each cup with a small piece of aluminum foil and poke a popsicle stick through the foil and into the cup. Freeze cups for 2 to 3 hours or until firm. To serve, remove foil and peel cup away from popsicle.

Serving size: *1 popsicle*
Calories: *89*
Fat: *1 g*

Frozen Mint Crème Cookie Yogurt

Makes 4 cups

8 Snackwell's Mint Crème Cookies, chopped
4 C. vanilla nonfat frozen yogurt, softened

In a medium bowl, stir cookie pieces into frozen yogurt. Freeze for 1 hour or until firm. Remove from freezer and scoop into small bowls to serve.

Serving size: *½ cup*
Calories: *90*
Fat: *2 g*

Simple Cranberry Sorbet

Makes 4 cups

3 C. low-calorie cranberry juice cocktail, divided
1 (.3 oz.) pkg. Jell-O sugar-free cranberry gelatin mix
1 C. cold evaporated skim milk

In a small saucepan over medium heat, bring 1½ cups juice to a boil. Stir hot juice into gelatin mix in a large bowl for 2 minutes or until completely dissolved. Stir in remaining juice and milk. Transfer to a 9 x 13″ baking pan; cover and freeze for 1½ hours or until frozen 1″ from edges of pan. Spoon mixture into a food processor or blender; cover and process until smooth but not melted. Pour into a 4- to 6-cup container with a lid; cover and freeze for 3 hours or until firm. To serve, let stand at room temperature for 5 minutes before scooping into small bowls.

Serving size: *1 cup*
Calories: *100*
Fat: *0 g*

Vanilla Berry Soy Popsicles

Makes 12 popsicles

2 C. blueberries
2 C. strawberries, hulled
½ C. brown sugar
2½ C. vanilla soy milk

Using a blender or food processor, puree blueberries and strawberries until smooth. Using a cheesecloth-lined sieve, strain berry juice into a medium bowl. Stir brown sugar into the juice. Add soy milk and stir until well blended. Divide mixture into 12 (3-ounce) plastic or paper cups. Cover each cup with a small piece of aluminum foil and poke a popsicle stick through the foil and into the cup. Freeze cups 2 to 3 hours or until firm. To serve, remove foil and peel cup away from popsicle.

Serving size: 1 popsicle
Calories: 98
Fat: 1.5 g

Beverages

Chocolate Almond Joe

Makes 1 cup

1 C. hot brewed coffee
1 T. Equal Spoonful
2 tsp. unsweetened cocoa powder
¼ tsp. almond extract

Combine coffee, Equal Spoonful, cocoa powder and almond extract in a coffee mug; stir until well blended. Serve coffee warm.

Serving size: *1 cup*
Calories: *19*
Fat: *1 g*

Feel the Burn!

Just 15 minutes of brisk walking will burn approximately 100 calories.

Fizzy Mango Frappé

1 whole ripe mango, peeled and pitted
¾ C. orange juice
¼ C. lime juice
1¼ C. club soda
2 ice cubes

In a food processor or blender, puree the mango. Add the orange juice and lime juice; process until smooth. Add the club soda and ice cubes; blend just until the ice is crushed. Pour into tall drink glasses and serve immediately.

Serving size: *1 cup*
Calories: *83*
Fat: *0 g*

Citrus Mango Punch

Makes 9 cups

6 C. cold water
2 C. mango nectar
1 C. orange juice
1 C. Splenda No Calorie Sweetener, granular
1 (.16 oz.) env. Kool-Aid unsweetened tropical punch

In a large pitcher, combine water, mango nectar, orange juice, Splenda and Kool-Aid. Stir until well combined and Splenda has dissolved. Serve in tall drinking glasses over ice.

Serving size: *1 cup*
Calories: *60*
Fat: *0 g*

Strawberry Tea

1 C. orange juice
¼ C. sugar
⅓ C. powdered instant tea
1 (10 oz.) pkg. frozen strawberries, thawed
4 C. water
2 C. crushed ice
Fresh lemon wedges, optional

In a blender, combine orange juice, sugar, tea and strawberries; blend until smooth. Pour mixture into a 2-quart pitcher; add water and ice. Serve tea in tall drinking glasses and garnish with a fresh lemon wedge if desired.

Serving size: *1 cup*
Calories: *81*
Fat: *0 g*

Frosty Strawberry Daiquiri

2 C. fresh strawberries
¼ C. frozen limeade concentrate
1 C. crushed ice
2 tsp. rum extract
Whole fresh strawberries, optional

In a blender, combine strawberries, frozen limeade, ice and rum extract; blend until smooth. Serve daiquiris in short drinking glasses and garnish with a fresh whole strawberry if desired.

Serving size: *¾ cup*
Calories: *48*
Fat: *0 g*

Spiced Veggie Cocktail

1 T. lime juice
1 qt. vegetable juice cocktail
2 tsp. Worcestershire sauce
Dash of pepper
Dash of Tabasco sauce
Fresh lemon slices, optional
Fresh celery stalks, optional

In a tall pitcher, combine lime juice, vegetable juice cocktail, Worcestershire sauce, pepper and Tabasco sauce; stir until well combined. Serve in tall drink glasses over ice. Garnish with lemon slices and celery stalks if desired.

Serving size: *1 cup*
Calories: *43*
Fat: *0 g*

Pineapple Cranberry Punch

1 (46 oz.) can pineapple juice
1 (46 oz.) bottle reduced-calorie cranberry juice cocktail
1 T. almond extract
2 qts. sugar-free lemon-lime soft drink

In a large mixing or punch bowl, combine pineapple juice, cranberry juice and almond extract; stir until well combined. Add lemon-lime soft drink just before serving.

Serving size: *¾ cup*
Calories: *54*
Fat: *0 g*

Feel the Burn!

Go ahead – jump! Jumping rope for 10 minutes will burn 100 calories.

Tomato Pepper Cocktail

Makes 6 cups

4 large tomatoes, quartered
1 small green bell pepper, chopped
1 small onion, chopped
1 stalk celery, chopped
1 T. sugar
½ tsp. pepper
¼ tsp. Tabasco sauce, optional
Celery leaves, optional

In a food processor or blender, combine tomatoes, green pepper, onion and celery; process until smooth. Pour mixture into a tall pitcher and stir in sugar, pepper and Tabasco sauce. Serve chilled in tall drink glasses. Garnish with celery leaves if desired.

Serving size: *¾ cup*
Calories: *29*
Fat: *0 g*

Strawberry
Banana Smoothie

Makes 5 cups

3 C. crushed ice
1 C. sliced fresh or frozen strawberries
1 medium banana, peeled and sliced
1 C. nonfat, sugar-free, strawberry yogurt

In a blender, combine ice, strawberries, banana and yogurt; puree 1 minute or until smooth. Serve smoothies in tall drinking glasses.

Serving size: *1¼ cups*
Calories: *80*
Fat: *0 g*

Chilled Orange Cappuccino

Makes 8 cups

Peel from one orange, cut into ½″ strips
7½ C. cold water
1½ C. drip-grind espresso coffee
3 to 4 T. NutraSweet Spoonful
3 C. skim milk
Lite Cool Whip, optional
Cocoa powder, ground nutmeg or cinnamon, optional

Place orange peel in the bottom of a coffee pot. Brew coffee using cold water and espresso. Once brewed, let coffee cool to room temperature and strain coffee; discard orange peel. Stir in NutraSweet Spoonful and skim milk. Refrigerate for 1 hour until chilled. Pour cappuccino into tall chilled drinking glasses and spoon one dollop of Lite Cool Whip on top of cappuccino. Sprinkle Cool Whip with cocoa powder, ground nutmeg or cinnamon.

Serving size: *1 cup*
Calories: *45*
Fat: *7 g*

Tasty Tip

Cappuccino can be frozen in ice-cube trays and used to chill warm coffee and add a little flavor. Or, cappuccino cubes can be crushed in a blender for a tasty smoothie.

Sweet Chai Tea

Makes 1 cup

½ C. hot brewed sweet orange tea
½ C. very warm fat-free or 2% milk
1 T. Equal Spoonful
¼ tsp. vanilla extract
⅛ tsp. ground cloves

Combine tea, milk, Equal Spoonful, vanilla extract and ground cloves in a coffee mug; stir until well combined. Serve tea immediately.

Serving size: *1 cup*
Calories: *53*
Fat: *0 g*

Feel the Burn!

Caffeine is a stimulant, and stimulants tend to increase the calories you burn. One likely reason is that they give you the short-term impression that you have more energy, which could mean you move more. Caffeine may also cause metabolic changes in the body that can result in more calories burned.

INDEX

Crunchy Munchies

Dips & Dippers

INDEX

Fruits & Vegetables

Feeling Fancy

INDEX

INDEX